beethoven

string quartet in A minor, opus 132

viola

MMO CD 4503

music minus one viola

Beethoven

String Quartet in A minor, Opus 132

4503

COMPACT DISC PAGE AND BAND INFORMATION

MMO CD 4503

Music Minus One

BEETHOVEN
Quintet in A Minor, Opus 132
Viola

Printed in Canada

3 taps (1 measure) precede music.

Allegro, ma non tanto

Heiliger Dankgesang eines Genesenen an die Gottheit, in der lydischen Tonart.
(Canzona di ringraziamento offerta alla divinità da un guarito, in modo lidico.)

Alla Marcia, assai vivace

4 taps (1 measure) precede music.

Più allegro

Violino.

Viola.